Celebrate Spring
Rain Showers

by Kathryn Clay

CAPSTONE PRESS
a capstone imprint

Little Pebble is published by Capstone Press,
1710 Roe Crest Drive, North Mankato, Minnesota 56003
www.mycapstone.com

Library of Congress Cataloging-in-Publication Data
Library of Congress Cataloging-in-Publication data is on file with the Library of Congress.
ISBN 978-1-4914-8303-9 (library binding)
ISBN 978-1-4914-8307-7 (paperback)
ISBN 978-1-4914-8311-4 (ebook PDF)

Editorial Credits
Erika L. Shores, editor; Juliette Peters and Ashlee Suker, designers;
Svetlana Zhurkin, media researcher; Katy LaVigne, production specialist

Photo Credits
iStockphoto: dennisjim, 9; Shutterstock: Aspen Photo, 15, Brian A. Jackson, 5, Gayvoronskaya_
Yana, 7, Geo Martinez, 20, georgemphoto, 11, Maksim Chaikou, 1, Marten_House, 19, Olha
Ukhal, 3, Patrick Foto, cover, Photo Fun, 17, Stacey Ann Alberts, 21, tab62, 13, USBFCO, back
cover and throughout

Table of Contents

Spring Is Here! 4

Rain Helps Plants 10

Rain Helps Animals. 14

After a Storm. 18

Glossary 22
Read More 23
Internet Sites 23
Index. 24

Spring Is Here!

Winter is over.

The days grow warmer.

Rainy spring weather is here.

Dark clouds roll in.

Lightning flashes.

Boom! Thunder bangs.

Tiny drops start to fall.

Heavy showers soak the ground.

Rain Helps Plants

Roots suck up the rain.

Stems poke from the dirt.

Leaves grow on the stems.

Flower buds grow.

Soon pink tulips bloom.

Rain Helps Animals

Rain makes puddles.

A thirsty deer takes a drink.

Worms die if they dry out.
Rain keeps their bodies wet.

After a Storm

Maya puts on boots.

She plays in the puddles.

The sun comes out.

Jackson sees a rainbow.

21

Glossary

bloom—to produce a flower

bud—part of a plant that turns into a leaf or flower

root—the part of a plant that attaches to the ground

stem—the main body of a plant